Busy Trains

A Random House PICTUREBACK®

Busy Trains

At the busy railroad station people wait for trains. Some of the trains will bring visitors from far-off cities. Others will carry people where they want to go. The next busy train leaves from Track Number 1. People hurry to the gate with their baggage. *All aboard!*

A trainman helps passengers onto the train. The conductor signals the engineer, who will wait until everyone is safely on board before he starts the engine. Passenger trains carry people and baggage. Freight trains carry all kinds of cargo—from coal to cows. Animals ride in the cattle car.

Trains with many cars are heavy. They need big, powerful engines to pull them. This steam-powered locomotive carries coal and water in a car called a tender. A fireman shovels coal into the firebox. As the coal burns it heats the water, making steam to power the engine. When the water supply runs low, the engineer stops at a water tower.

Some trains have just a few cars. Others may have hundreds! Look out the window. There are three busy trains. On an overnight passenger train, travelers relax in private roomettes or watch the sights from the lounge car's dome. Some people sleep in sleeping cars. The steam engine is pulling a cattle car, a side dumper, and a box car.

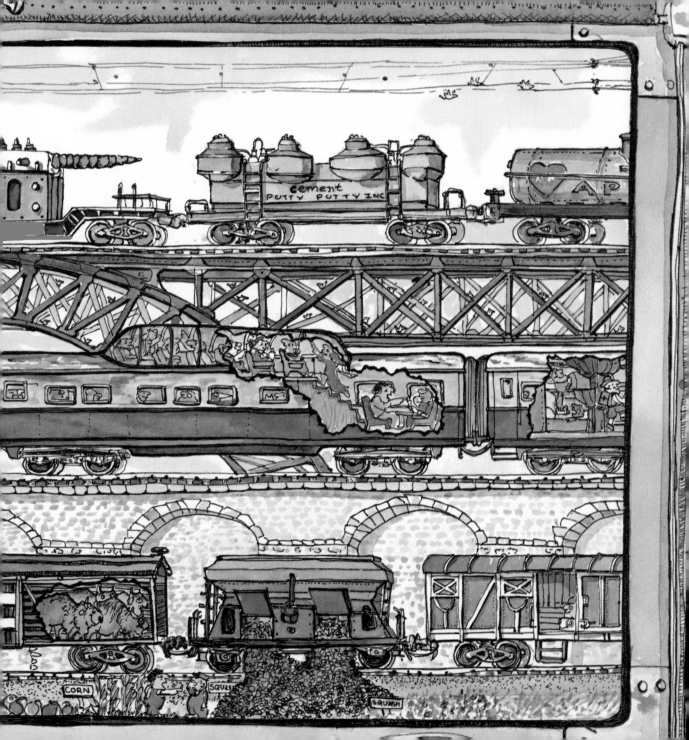

Big cargo containers hold all kinds of freight—coffee or furniture, pianos or toys. Containers can be carried on trains, in ships, and on trucks. They don't have to be unpacked every time they are moved, so they save time and work. A huge rig puts the container on a freight-train flatcar.

An electric locomotive pulls a long freight train. Its tank cars carry liquids like oil or chemicals. Passenger trains usually have a dining car. This one has a mail car too, where postal workers sort letters. Most freight trains have a caboose at the end, where the crew can relax when they take a break.

Early steam engines burned wood instead of coal. One of the first was a little engine called the "Puffing Billy." Many of these old locomotives are now in train museums.

To warn people and animals to stay away from the tracks, some locomotives had bright headlights and loud whistles. Others had bumpers in front, called cowcatchers, which kept the tracks clear of debris.

Most locomotives today are run by diesel fuel or electricity.

Many electric trains get power from a special electric rail that runs along the tracks. Others use overhead electrical cables like these. Repair cars have high platforms where workers can stand when they have to fix the cables. A special car carries big spools of new cable.

Speedy electric commuter trains take people from small towns to work in big cities. In a tunnel, a red signal light tells the engineer in the cab to stop.

She waits until the other train is out
of sight. When it is far away, the
light will turn green. Then the
engineer knows it is safe to go on.

Special trains do special jobs. Busy little mining trains bring ore out of the mine. Side-tipping cars dump loads of ore onto waiting barges.

At the steel mill, hot liquid metal is poured into special tank cars with many wheels. The top of another kind of car tips open to take in a hot metal bar called an ingot.

When a diesel locomotive needs repairs, it goes to a diesel repair shed. In the repair shed, workers get busy trains ready for more work. One locomotive gets a coat of fresh paint. An overhead crane lifts a locomotive off its wheels. Workers use blowtorches to fix the wheel section. Another crane lifts out the diesel engine itself so the workers can clean and repair it.

The repair sheds stand in a large circle around a huge turntable. It points the cars to one of the sheds. There is a locomotive on the turntable now. The workers have just fixed its engine. They put grease and oil on its moving parts to keep it running smoothly. When the turntable stops turning, the locomotive will go down a track and out of the yard. After its bath with showers of hot water, the other car will be ready to go back to work.

ENGINE REPAIR

Accidents can sometimes happen if tracks, signals, bridges, and equipment are not kept in good repair.

Luckily no one was hurt when this railroad bridge collapsed.

Railroad cranes will lift the cars back onto the tracks. A railroad inspector tries to find out what caused the wreck. She will make sure that the bridge is quickly repaired.

Taking good care of the tracks can prevent train accidents. A special engine can find dangerous cracks in the rails. A track worker uses a smaller machine to check for cracks, too. Cranes place a whole section of new track in position. Wooden crossties support the rails. When they need to be replaced, a tie remover raises the rails and pushes out the old ties. Other machines dig ditches and smooth out gravel around the tracks.

Trains must keep running, night and day, in good weather and bad weather. In the winter, a snow plow rides along the rails, blowing snow off the railroad tracks. It keeps the tracks clear so that busy trains can always get through.